Brittany's Accomplishments

By

Martha V. Bradford

Illustrations By

Phillip Tinnin, Sr.

authorHOUSE™

1663 Liberty Drive, Suite 200
Bloomington, Indiana 47403
(800) 839-8640
www.AuthorHouse.com

First published by AuthorHouse 111/05/04

ISBN: 1-4208-9984-8 (e)
ISBN: 1-4208-9985-6 (sc)

Printed in the United States of America
Bloomington, Indiana

This book is printed on acid-free paper.

Acknowledgments

This book is about a little seven-year-old black American girl who is blind, and has overcome and accomplished the things that she most feared. She is a great pianist and composes all her own music, since the age of four.

This book is a dedication to my granddaughter who was born blind, and is a very intelligent, bright young lady. I have learned a lot from her as she has learned a lot from life. When she was younger, she would get frustrated at times, not understanding why things happened the way they did. Now she realizes that she is a gift from God, and said, "God made everyone special and God does not make mistakes."

She is my inspiration. I admire the strength that she has shown throughout her years. I would like this children's book to inspire all children. Whatever goals you want to accomplish out of life, you have to want it bad enough, first of all. And then you have to work really hard to accomplish it.

I hope Brittany's Accomplishments *will inspire others as it has me. Without her, I would not been able to write this book. I was inspired by the greatness of this gifted child and the grace of God. She has shown me that there is no limit, just set your goals and work hard to accomplish them. I have written a poem that reflects the strengths to go on and push for better things in your life; it's called "I Must Go On." I always refer to my poem when things get rough.*

I would like to thank Phillip L. Tinnin, Sr. for the beautiful illustrations. He is a great, talented artist, and I would like to see him accomplish his goals in life. Also I would like to thank the Children's Center for the Visually Impaired for being a great asset in my life and for giving all the love and support to my family and me.

THE RECITAL

Martha V. Bradford

This is a story about a little girl who didn't want to study or practice on her music, but she wanted to be the best.

The little girl's name was Brittany. She was seven years old. She was born blind and was very smart. She played the piano, and she was great. She played classical and jazz. She played by ear and had been playing since she was four years old. She also composed her own pieces and they were beautiful.

When it came time for her to practice making her pieces perfect, she never wanted to practice. She said that her mother was being too hard on her, making her practice so much.

Brittany wanted to be the best music composer in the world, and had promised to practice on a daily basis. She would come in from school and play each piece that she had composed once, and would speed through them. Once she sped through them, she would go on playing her favorite tunes that she had just heard or the tunes from a song that was sung in her music class at school.

Brittany was told if she didn't practice her music that she wouldn't get to go to the amusement park with her mom.

She would come home from school and practice daily on her music. She was playing her pieces beautifully. Her mom decided to take her to the studio to let her record her music. Then she would be able to put her music on the market, so that everyone would be able to enjoy it.

Her mother told her she had to work especially hard to be able to play her music with no mistakes. She had to keep the pieces the same and not change the chords around. "Everything must stay as you have first played it," her mother said.

Brittany felt overwhelmed and felt she couldn't do what her mom wanted her to do, so she fell back and stopped practicing again. She didn't want to play her favorite tunes anymore, nor did she compose any new pieces. She just felt she couldn't handle what her mom was asking of her.

While sitting at her desk, Brittany thought, "I can't do what my mom has asked of me. It is too hard, not making any mistakes. What if I mess up really bad, and no one will like my music?"

Her mother did not say anything to her. She just let Brittany do whatever she wanted to do. She never reminded her about the amusement park outing. On the night before they were to go on the outing, Brittany asked her mother what time they were going.

Her mom said, "Going where?"

"You know, you had promised an amusement park outing for us, so what time are we going?"

"Brittany, I told you that if you didn't work really hard on your music, we would not be going. You did great for a couple of days and you just stopped. I was wondering if you were just taking a break. But you never went back to practicing. You always said you wanted to be the best. It takes practice to make perfect. If you want to excel in anything, it takes hard work."

Her mom said, "You have to want it bad enough, and also you have to work on it. It doesn't come to you overnight, or just drop in your lap. You have to work at it. Do you remember when you first started playing the piano? You were playing basic songs. You didn't know the notes or anything, so you worked on it."

"But Mom, I just don't feel that I'm good enough to record my music for others to be interested. I love playing and composing my music, but I just don't think it's good enough for others to enjoy."

"Oh, Brittany, I didn't know you felt that way. I know
what we could do to make you think different. Let's put on
a show with just family and close friends. We will serve
refreshments, and also have your cousin Tre and your cousin
Michael to perform. They can do a rap song and dance. Your
friend Sharonda can also play the piano. She plays pretty
good, and it will be great."

"Mom, that will be great," said Brittany. "Can I play three of
my pieces and my favorite, 'The Powerpuff Girls'? I'd like to
sing 'The Powerpuff Girls' too."

"Brittany, that would be fine. Let's get to work on this
recital."

The day of the recital, Mom and Brittany moved the table from the dining room and set up the chairs and waited for the guests to arrive. They had cookies, cake, punch, cheese, and crackers. Everything was set up so nice.

"Hello, Aunt Brenda, Aunt Tish, and Aunt Debbie. Glad you could make it. Mom is in the kitchen," Brittany said.

Mom said, "Hello, glad you could make it this afternoon. We are going to put on a great show for you, and we hope you will enjoy it. First we are going to have Sharonda play two of her favorite songs on the piano, and then Tre and Michael are going to rap for us. Then Brittany will play three pieces that she has composed. They all are great and they have worked really hard to put on this show. So enjoy the show."

Sharonda played "Winnie the Pooh" and "Twinkle Twinkle Little Star." She did not play with a lot of confidence, but she did well. Everyone enjoyed her efforts and praised her for a job well done. Tre and Michael sang along with a rap tape and danced beautifully. They did a great job. They were also praised after their performance.

Brittany played three of her pieces that she had composed. She only made a couple of mistakes, but went on playing. She felt good about her playing. She also played "The Powerpuff Girls" and sang along. Brittany had a great voice. She sang with confidence. She was great and everyone praised her performance also.

The show went with a blast. Everyone enjoyed it. They all were great. Everyone stood up and clapped for the performers. The children were so happy that everyone liked the show. They even spoke of giving another show.

Mom said, "That's great. We will work on doing this again. But first we need to get you ready to record in the studio."

Brittany worked very hard in the next few weeks and was ready to record her first CD.

She recorded a CD with eleven of her songs that she had composed, and sold lots of CDs. They were also sold from the neighborhood stores. It was a big hit. Everyone loved her CD because she was a very special little girl.

With the money that she had made from the CD, she donated to a non-profit organization for blind children, like herself.

Soon, Brittany was thinking about making another CD. She had overcome the negative thoughts of not being able to do what she loved doing best.

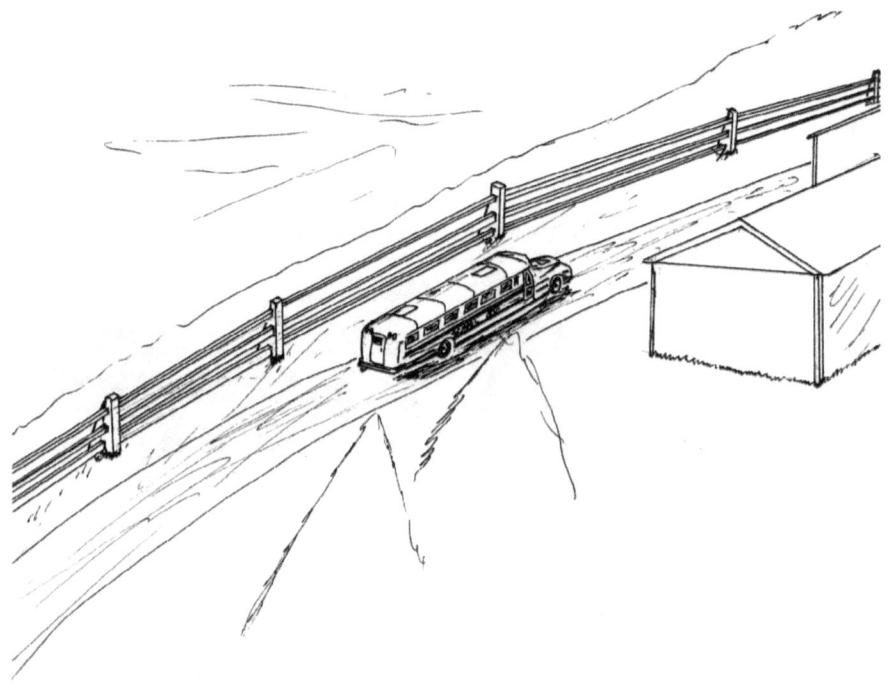

Brittany loved getting up in the morning and getting ready for school. She dressed herself in the mornings with little help from Mom. She attended a regular school with sighted children. She got along great with all of the children.

While eating her breakfast one day, Brittany said to her mom, "We are going on a field trip today at school and I really don't want to go. We are going to the horse stables and I'm not too fond of horses. Do I have to go?"

"Yes, Brittany. You can't miss school because you don't like the field trip that you're going on."

Brittany arrived at school and was in deep thought, just thinking about the horses, hoping that she didn't have to ride them.

"Mrs. Brown," Brittany said, "I am afraid of horses. Do I have to go on this field trip?"

"Yes, Brittany. I want you to go with the class. You have to overcome your fear of horses and other animals. I want you to go and enjoy yourself. We will have a great time."

"OK, Mrs. Brown. I will try to enjoy the field trip, as long as I don't have to ride any horses."

"Oh, Brittany, you will enjoy riding the horses. It's the greatest feeling."

It was time for the children to board the bus. Brittany was kind of excited. Her friend Dana asked if she was going to ride the horses. "I don't think I will," Brittany said. "I hate the noises that the horses make, and they are so big and scary."

Martha V. Bradford

The owner of the stables greeted the children. Mrs. Brown introduced all the children to the stable owner. He was excited to meet everyone. He showed them around the stables and explained how he cared for the horses daily. The children were excited and ready to start riding.

Mrs. Brown said, "OK, we are going to get on our horses now and ride the trails.

Brittany, are you ready? There will be a guide for you. The guide will ride next to you and guide your horse along with his horse."

Brittany was afraid, but she got on the horse anyway.

Martha V. Bradford

"Oh! This is fun. I like riding this horse," Brittany said with excitement. And everyone laughed with joy and was happy to see Brittany enjoy her first horse ride.

After the long ride through the trail, the children had lunch on the picnic grounds of the stables. Brittany was so excited, she asked, "Could we ride the trail again after lunch?"

"No," Mrs. Brown said, "we will be boarding the bus soon." Then Mrs. Brown said, Brittany, I'm surprised. You have really overcome your fear of horses."

Brittany said, "I just love riding the horses, but I don't want them to lick me because they have such a big mouth and teeth. Maybe we can come back again to ride the horses one day."

Brittany arrived home. She couldn't wait to tell her mom what she had done. "Oh, Mom," she said, "I rode a horse and I love riding horses now."

"That's great, Brittany. I knew you would do it and enjoy it."

About The Author

Martha is a young grandmother who is raising (2) two of her grandchildren. She enjoys raising her grandchildren, that's where her strength and motivation comes from. She dedicated her book to her granddaughter who is blind and is a very intellegent young lady, who is actually a pianist that composes her own music. This is where she got her inspiration to write this book. To hear her granddaughter at the age if five to express how God does not make mistakes and that he made everyone special. This comment came after being teased about being different.